20 Promises with Biblical Proof by
Nathaniel E. Jones

Copyright © 2017 by Nathaniel E. Jones

All rights reserved. This book or any portion thereof may not be reproduced or used in any manner whatsoever without the express written permission of the publisher except for the use of brief quotations in a book review or scholarly journal.

Unless otherwise indicated all scripture quotations are taken from the Holy Bible, New International Version, NIV Copyright © 1973, 1978, 1984, 2011 by Biblica, Inc. Used by permission. All rights reserved worldwide.

Printed in the United States of America.

First Printing: 2017

ISBNs: 978-0-578-21339-2 (2018), 978-1-387-30825-5 (2017)

Camden County, NJ.

U.S. trade bookstores and wholesalers: Nathaniel Jones, njoneseastern@gmail.com.

Table of Contents

20 Promises with Biblical Proof by Nathaniel E. Jones..............................i

Preface..1

1. *Breakthrough* **Joshua 5:6-7.** God disciplines you before you enter the promise land, be obedient in the process...3

2. *Reward* **Joshua 24:11-16.** Let God prepare you for what he has for you. Serve God to set an example for others...4

3. *Change* **Deuteronomy 2:1-3.** Look for God to shift your season. Stay away from sinful habits and trust in the people God sends to help you......................6

4. *Mercy* **Psalm 145:8-21.** Believe the things God tells you will happen. Hold on to the promises within his word. Stay away from sin and let God lead you...7

5. *Deliverance* **Believe God to fight for you and cause hard seasons to end. Expect to get more than what your enemies have held back from you**...10

6. *Direction* **Joshua 8:3-4.** Listen to God's instructions and be alert. Sometimes you must use cunning to defeat an enemy. Some battles are won in prayer...11

7. *Victory* **Joshua 14:6-11.** Expect an inheritance and follow God in every circumstance. Victory comes through patience and letting God see you through problems...12

8. *Provision* **Deuteronomy 8:3-10.** Look forward to God changing your circumstances at an appointed time. Become more mature so you can handle provision..14

9. *Peace* **Psalm 23:1-4.** God can remove the threat of defeat or loss. Sometimes, the attacks of your enemies must be withheld to have peace....................16

10. *Confidence* **Psalm 46:1 KJV** *God is our refuge and strength, a very present help in trouble.* When you cannot handle a problem yourself God intervenes..18

11. *Manifestation* **Let the trial leave you internally and it will manifest on the outside.** Seek the kingdom of God and expect the deliverance you need..20

12. *Guidance* **Isaiah 4:2-6.** If you stay where you are with an obedient attitude, blessings come. Let God guide you in every area of your life. Seek God's wisdom and live in purity..22

13. *Completion* **1 Samuel 30:1-8.** God's will is recorded in the Bible. People cannot change what God accomplished. The number three is used by God in many instances in the Bible and has significance to God completing something....24

14. *Prosperity* God wants you to be prosperous in every area. Expect God to bless your relationships, health, and business endeavors..............................26

15. *Diligence* Let God teach you how to prioritize your time. God will bless your hard work if you study and prepare correctly. God can use you with any degree or amount of experience……………………………………………………………..29

16. *Promotion* **Psalm 75.** Humility proceeds honor and God blesses those with the right attitude. Believe God to promote you in the right timing. This promotion may be deliverance, healing, a new job, a wife, a husband, or a new house……..30

17. *Courage* **Joshua 10:1-16.** Be bold and speak to your mountains. Rebuke fear and trust in the Lord. God can sustain. Keep still and allow God to see you through trials…………..32

18. *Renewal* **Romans 12.** God wants to reign in your mind and give you peace. God can repay you for any hardship or struggles. There are hard seasons in life, but there are also good seasons. God wants there to be breaks from trials in your life……………………………………………………………………………….36

19. *Harvest* **Proverbs 11 KJV** *A false balance is abomination to the LORD: but a just weight is his delight.* God has a just weight in store for those who are obedient. God rewards hard work and consistency. Believe God to reward your acts of service……………………………………………………………………………..38

20. *Payback* **Proverbs 24.** People do not get away with sin. Expect God to defend you. At the same time, you must forgive those who wrong you. God can make up for the past. Believe the Lord for recovery and restoration……………………….40

Preface

The purpose of this book is to influence change in your life. Each chapter presents a teaching that is transformative and encouraging. The focus of this book is to help you move forward in life and anticipate the promises and provision of God. God is Alpha and Omega, "the beginning and the end" (Revelation 22:13). We all can reflect on the things God accomplishes for us in the beginning of our life, but often we forget that he has a road ahead of us. This road can be heaven, or a more abundant life on earth.

The Bible talks about how faith can move mountains. Faith also involves speaking. For example, when Elijah prayed, rain came down upon the earth (1 Kings 18). Material in this book will encourage you to move forward and empower you to make decisions. Jeremiah 29:11 mentions that God has an "expected end." The expected end is whatever word God speaks over you in advance. Before the word manifests in the natural, there is a process that you must go through. Waiting on God can be a trial. When you use the word of God properly, you can empower yourself just by meditating and reading scriptures. My aim is to interpret the Bible in a modern way that can relate to difficulties within a Christian's life.

1. Breakthrough

Joshua 5:6-7 KJV For the children of Israel walked forty years in the wilderness, till all the people that were men of war, which came out of Egypt, were consumed, because they obeyed not the voice of the LORD: unto whom the LORD sware that he would not shew them the land, which the LORD sware unto their fathers that he would give us, a land that floweth with milk and honey. 7 And their children, whom he raised up in their stead, them Joshua circumcised: for they were uncircumcised, because they had not circumcised them by the way.

People who were disobedient did not make it into the promise land. The descendants of the children of Israel moved forward. God will not give his people anything that they cannot handle. Sometimes God may use you to lead others to victory, but we must be obedient to instructions.

Waiting and obedience leads to breakthrough in your life. God may be looking for you to keep still. Trust God to release any burdens that plague your mind and heart. What you believe by faith becomes visible. There can't be great struggle without a great comeback. The end is always better than the beginning (Ecclesiastes 7:8).

1. Rebuke the spirit of fear and it will leave you (2 Timothy 1:7).

2. Be obedient and believe God to give you more for your struggle.

2. Reward

Joshua 24:11-16 NIV

11 Then you crossed the Jordan and came to Jericho. The citizens of Jericho fought against you, as did also the Amorites, Perizzites, Canaanites, Hittites, Girgashites, Hivites and Jebusites, but I gave them into your hands.

God will allow you to defeat every enemy you encounter.

12 I sent the hornet ahead of you, which drove them out before you—also the two Amorite kings. You did not do it with your own sword and bow.

Before God moves you into new territory, A path must be prepared. God can send angels to fight for you. Like hornets they can fly and attack. As small as hornets are people fear them. Early in the beginning of Genesis angels guard the tree of life (Genesis 3:24). In 2 Kings 19:35 an angel kills 185,000 men. One purpose of angels is to protect and fight. Believe God to fight your battles.

13 So I gave you a land on which you did not toil and cities you did not build; and you live in them and eat from vineyards and olive groves that you did not plant.

God can give you the spoils of a battle you do not fight. The only fighting that is needed is the declaration of promises and prayer. Read your Bible and declare the words of Jesus.

God always prepares his blessings. If God gave you an unprepared blessing, one of two things could happen; (1) you could lose it, (2) you wouldn't be able to handle what God grants you so it would be bad.

14 "Now fear the Lord and serve him with all faithfulness. Throw away the gods your ancestors worshiped beyond the Euphrates River and in Egypt, and serve the Lord.

15 But if serving the Lord seems undesirable to you, then choose for yourselves this day whom you will serve, whether the gods your ancestors served beyond the Euphrates, or the gods of the Amorites, in whose land you are living. But as for me and my household, we will serve the Lord.
16 Then the people answered, "Far be it from us to forsake the Lord to serve other god's!

Serve Jesus with all your heart, soul, and mind. He will reward you. When you serve the Lord, you set an example for others in your household. This household may be your family, your friends, or your coworkers.
Don't serve foreign Gods. Make sure your actions, intentions, and thoughts worship God. Without faithful and consistent service to God you risk being influenced to serve false gods.

3. Change

Just because you cannot see breakthrough does not mean it's won't come. Get ready for change in whatever area of life you need it.

1. If you forgive your enemies God will take responsibility for them (Deuteronomy 32:35).
2. Do not worry about how to make decisions properly. God can grant people to give guidance (Proverbs 11:14).

Deuteronomy 2:1-3 NIV

1 Then we turned back and set out toward the wilderness along the route to the Red Sea, as the LORD had directed me. For a long time we made our way around the hill country of Seir. 2 Then the LORD said to me, 3 "You have made your way around this hill country long enough; now turn north.

Stay away from sinful habits. God does not want to grant you blessings when you keep an old mindset. Stay along the path God has placed you on and don't turn back.

If you're tired, it could be a sign that God wants to shift your location. You may not stay in the same circumstances in life whether good or bad. There are times and seasons and both the righteous and the unrighteous experience rain and sun (Matthew 5:45). God allows seasons to change. Look for God's goodness in whatever season you are in.

Sometimes it may feel like you are losing the battle, but the Lord is coming to save you. All things work to the good (Romans 8:28). God's desires to shift circumstances in your favor.

4. Mercy

Psalm 145:8-21 NLT

8 The Lord is merciful and compassionate,
slow to get angry and filled with unfailing love.
9 The Lord is good to everyone.
He showers compassion on all his creation.
10 All of your works will thank you, Lord,
and your faithful followers will praise you.

Everything you do both good and bad, God judges. Fortunately, he is full of grace and mercy. Anything you are doing wrong he can forgive. Actions made outside God's will are judged (Ecclesiastes 12:13-14). People do not realize that poor decisions can have a negative impact on the world. Make sure you leave a positive impact so God will be pleased with you. Faithful followers bless the Lord no matter what the circumstance. Be faithful to God and offer your praise.

11 They will speak of the glory of your kingdom;
they will give examples of your power.
12 They will tell about your mighty deeds
and about the majesty and glory of your reign.
13 For your kingdom is an everlasting kingdom.
You rule throughout all generations.

The Lord always keeps his promises;
he is gracious in all he does.
14 The Lord helps the fallen
and lifts those bent beneath their loads.
15 The eyes of all look to you in hope;
you give them their food as they need it.

Timing is not a problem for God because he can control timing. Jesus escaped dying early when people had the intent to kill him (John 8:59).

16 When you open your hand,
you satisfy the hunger and thirst of every living thing.

God does not just open his hands to feed us, but he uses them to lead and protect us. We have hands, and can give direction, so why wouldn't God. You may be dealing with consequences of sin or the mistakes of others, but Jesus is pointing you in the right direction. Keep walking and don't stop. You will experience God's promises and breakthrough on the way.

17 The Lord is righteous in everything he does;
he is filled with kindness.
18 The Lord is close to all who call on him,
yes, to all who call on him in truth.
19 He grants the desires of those who fear him;
he hears their cries for help and rescues them.
20 The Lord protects all those who love him,
but he destroys the wicked.

21 I will praise the Lord,
and may everyone on earth bless his holy name
forever and ever.

Trust God to:

1. Deal with evildoers.

2. Provide protection.

3. Give you the desires of your heart.

Do not think about your problems, meditate on the goodness of Jesus and his ability to solve problems. If you think Jesus isn't solving a problem, he works around a problem sometimes. God accomplishes his will in both ways. Believe the things God tells you will happen.

5. Deliverance

Isaiah 35:4 KJV "Say to them that are of a fearful heart, Be strong, fear not: behold, your God will come with vengeance, even God with a recompence; he will come and save you.

Get ready for your time. The time for possessing things you want is coming and the wait may not be much longer if you believe and trust God.

Expect to get more than what the enemy has held back from you.

Ecclesiastes 12:13-14 KJV Let us hear the conclusion of the whole matter: Fear God, and keep his commandments: for this is the whole duty of man. 14 For God shall bring every work into judgment, with every secret thing, whether it be good, or whether it be evil.

Sometimes God delivers swiftly. You may not know the day or hour, but when God moves, the wait is over. God promises to bring everything into judgement. Do not think people who do wrong will get away with it. There are consequences for everything except keeping godly commandments. There may be situations you are dealing with that are the fault of someone else, but God can change things rapidly. Believe God for deliverance.

6. Direction

Joshua 8:3-4 NIV So Joshua and the whole army moved out to attack Ai. He chose thirty thousand of his best fighting men and sent them out at night with these orders: "Listen carefully. You are to set an ambush behind the city. Don't go very far from it. All of you be on the alert.

There are three steps to take when dealing with an enemy:

1. Listen to God's instructions. Be aware that he's fighting on your behalf. When God tells you how to handle a situation listen.
2. Expect to win despite the circumstance you are in.

People who are righteous encounter difficulty, but God can deliver you each time.

3. Let prayer, and fasting take control of your life.

Prayer is a method of ambushing the enemy. One reason God speaks to people through dreams is because Satan can't see what God shows us while we are resting. In prayer, sometimes we are quite but God knows what we are saying. When you pray listen for God's voice. To receive directions from a person one must hear what is being said. Sometimes we do not perceive or recognize that God is speaking (Job 33:14).

7. Victory

Joshua 14:6-11 NIV, 6 Now the people of Judah approached Joshua at Gilgal, and Caleb son of Jephunneh the Kenizzite said to him, "You know what the LORD said to Moses the man of God at Kadesh Barnea about you and me. 7 I was forty years old when Moses the servant of the LORD sent me from Kadesh Barnea to explore the land. And I brought him back a report according to my convictions, 8 but my fellow Israelites who went up with me made the hearts of the people melt in fear. I, however, followed the LORD my God wholeheartedly. 9 So on that day Moses swore to me, 'The land on which your feet have walked will be your inheritance and that of your children forever, because you have followed the LORD my God wholeheartedly.

10 "Now then, just as the LORD promised, he has kept me alive for forty-five years since the time he said this to Moses, while Israel moved about in the wilderness. So here I am today, eighty-five years old! 11 I am still as strong today as the day Moses sent me out; I'm just as vigorous to go out to battle now as I was then.

Life is unpredictable, but God works all things to the good (Romans 8:28). If things have been going wrong for a while, expect a turn around.

    Follow God wholeheartedly because the devil wants your heart to melt in fear. David encouraged himself in God and sought guidance, this caused him to win. The Amalekites had raided Ziklag, capturing the women and children of David and his men. David sought the Lord and recovered everything the Amalekites had taken (1 Samuel 30:1-20). You can recover lost things.

Whether you're young or old God can do great things for you. Sometimes when God seemingly takes a long time to respond he has great things in store for you. You must preserve your faith when you wait. Prayer and patience can make time pass quickly. As you grow spiritually, you adapt to God's time table. A Christian ought to have more patience than unbelievers. God can redeem you from anything and grant you victory.

Believe God to help you win the battles of life.

8. Provision

Look forward to God changing your circumstances at the appointed time. God is true to his word and keeps his promises. What we call a trial God calls a test. God may use hard times to test your faith. The devil's plot aids in receiving what God has for us. God conquers Satan's obstacles and still gets his will done.
Deuteronomy 8:3-10 NIV

3 He humbled you, causing you to hunger and then feeding you with manna, which neither you nor your ancestors had known, to teach you that man does not live on bread alone but on every word that comes from the mouth of the LORD.

The Word of God is our main source. Fasting demonstrates your desire for God. Giving up a meal is a demonstration of sacrifice for God.

4-5 Your clothes did not wear out and your feet did not swell during these forty years. Know then in your heart that as a man disciplines his son, so the LORD your God disciplines you.

God preserves you in waiting and disciplines you in other areas besides what you are waiting for. Become more mature so you can handle God's provision.

6 Observe the commands of the LORD your God, walking in obedience to him and revering him. For the LORD your God is bringing you into a good land—a land with brooks, streams, and deep springs gushing out into the valleys and hills;

Follow what God tells you. Obedience leads to receiving provision. Good deeds lead to good things in God's kingdom.

8-9 A land with wheat and barley, vines and fig trees, pomegranates, olive oil and honey; a land where bread will not be scarce and you will lack nothing; a land where the rocks are iron and you can dig copper out of the hills.

God wants you to dig copper by finding financial provision in business endeavors. God provides the hills but we must dig out the blessings.

10 When you have eaten and are satisfied, praise the LORD your God for the good land he has given you.

Praise God in advance for what he will do and is doing. God can move in days, weeks, and months in the areas you wait. You may not have to wait years. Keep praying and don't give up.

9. Peace

Psalm 23:1-4 NIV

1 The LORD is my shepherd, I lack nothing.

You will lack nothing, everything you are worried about God is solving. If the process you go through to receive a blessing is hard, God can repay you for the struggle.

2 He makes me lie down in green pastures,
he leads me beside quiet waters,
3 he refreshes my soul.
he guides me along the right paths
   for his name's sake.

God will give guidance when you can't seem to hear his voice. You can go to church being led. The desires God gives us, leads to purpose in our lives. A consistent desire paired with peace is often God. There is fulfillment in truly doing the will of God for your life. The refreshing of your soul is connected to your obedience to the plans of God. This does not mean that you must be perfect, but intentionally seeking God's plans fulfills the soul.

4 Even though I walk
   through the darkest valley,
I will fear no evil,
   for you are with me;
your rod and your staff,
   they comfort me.

If you are walking through darkness in life, he's covering you with protection. A rod has a hook. God can hook somethings you need that you cannot access. A staff can be used for guidance and to assist in walking. Trust God to lead you in the right direction and help you move forward.

God will remove the threat of defeat or loss. Sometimes to receive peace the attacks of the enemy must be withheld. Although life is hard, the devil is limited in his power. The ability of God to prosper you cannot be stopped.

Allow God to lead you in the right direction. God sees everything, especially the things we do not see. Difficulty develops skills you can use later. This is the reason why God will take you on a difficult path. Believe God to calm and silence storms, giving you peace.

10. Confidence

Psalm 46 KJV

1 God is our refuge and strength, a very present help in trouble.

2 Therefore will not we fear, though the earth be removed, and though the mountains be carried into the midst of the sea.

When you cannot handle a problem yourself, God intervenes. God finds a way of protecting his people amid natural disasters. This is seen when you read the story of Noah in Genesis 6-9. God sometimes permits natural disasters but can control them. God brought a flood upon the earth because of the wickedness of humanity but protected Noah. Disasters that hit other people may miss you.

3 Though the waters thereof roar and be troubled, though the mountains shake with the swelling thereof. Selah.

4 There is a river, the streams whereof shall make glad the city of God, the holy place of the tabernacles of the most high.

5 God is in the midst of her; she shall not be moved: God shall help her, and that right early.

8 The heathen raged, the kingdoms were moved: he uttered his voice, the earth melted.

    Humility proceeds honor (Proverbs 18:12), If you want honor you must be willing to be humbled by God. God melted the earth. If you read Genesis 2:7 God formed humans from the dust of the ground. We are part of the earth.

7 The LORD of hosts is with us; the God of Jacob is our refuge. Selah.

8 Come, behold the works of the LORD, what desolations he hath made in the earth.

9 He maketh wars to cease unto the end of the earth; he breaketh the bow, and cutteth the spear in sunder; he burneth the chariot in the fire.

10 Be still, and know that I am God: I will be exalted among the heathen, I will be exalted in the earth.

Wars are going to cease. Whatever your battling will end. Breakthrough can invite a struggle but you can overcome any struggle with God. When an attack from the enemy is too strong he breaks the bow and spear.

The Lord is always exalted and if someone's actions are contrary to his will, he will humble them. God discourages people who are proud and full of selfish ambition. Let God handle your enemies.

11 The LORD of hosts is with us; the God of Jacob is our refuge. Selah.

Do not think God has forgotten what you've been through. Believe God for payback in money, relationships, and favor. Shame is for your enemies, not you. If your confidence is in God you will not to be ashamed (Psalm 118:8).

11. Manifestation

Matthew 6:33 KJV *Seek ye first the kingdom of God, and his righteousness; and all these things shall be added unto you.*

We should put adding in God's hands. Some people seek what they desire more than they do God. The result is always failure. Whatever you cannot get yourself, God can draw to you. Let the fear of defeat and loss leave you and trust in God's power.

Matthew 6:34 NIV *Therefore do not worry about tomorrow, for tomorrow will worry about itself. Each day has enough trouble of its own.*

God will take care of every challenge you encounter.

Deuteronomy 31:8 NIV *The Lord himself goes before you and will be with you; he will never leave you nor forsake you. Do not be afraid; do not be discouraged."*

Do not be afraid or discouraged. God will handle your enemies and deliver you from problems that cease to end.

Acts 2:17-21 NIV

17 In the last days, God says,

I will pour out my Spirit on all people.

Your sons and daughters will prophesy,

your young men will see visions,

your old men will dream dreams.

18 Even on my servants, both men and women,

I will pour out my Spirit in those days,

and they will prophesy.

19 I will show wonders in the heavens above

and signs on the earth below,

blood and fire and billows of smoke.

20 The sun will be turned to darkness

and the moon to blood

before the coming of the great and glorious day of the Lord.

21 And everyone who calls

on the name of the Lord will be saved.

Whatever you are going through, you may be in the last days. You just don't know God's timing. God may move at an unexpected time. Ten years, twenty years, five years, may not be in equation. Things could end this year for you. We do not always know the details of God's will, but his plans always prevail. When God speaks, change occurs.

God rewards people who spread his word. God can lead you to the right people and places to deliver the word. The plagues of Egypt were not just to help deliver the Israelites but also to show the wonders of God. God uses wonders as a visible example to strengthen our faith.

Your dreams are going to happen. Your visions will happen. Your promises will be fulfilled. God can bless you while you are waiting for something not just afterwards. Inward deliverance can come before outward deliverance. Sometimes God will shape your character and mental well-being before he answers your prayers or delivers you from a trial.

12. Guidance

Isaiah 4:2-6 NIV In that day the Branch of the LORD will be beautiful and glorious, and the fruit of the land will be the pride and glory of the survivors in Israel. 3 Those who are left in Zion, who remain in Jerusalem, will be called holy, all who are recorded among the living in Jerusalem. 4 The Lord will wash away the filth of the women of Zion; he will cleanse the bloodstains from Jerusalem by a spirit of judgment and a spirit of fire. 5 Then the LORD will create over all of Mount Zion and over those who assemble there a cloud of smoke by day and a glow of flaming fire by night; over everything the glory will be a canopy. 6 It will be a shelter and shade from the heat of the day, and a refuge and hiding place from the storm and rain.

God wants you to come out of trials with greater glory. Glory involves holiness, not living a sinful life. As Roman 3:23 says, we all fall short of the glory of God but as we become more like God sinful habits and issues should decrease.

Trials can cause your confidence in yourself, and God, to plummet. God can make up for the past. Some people leave where they are because of difficulty. If you stay where you are with obedience, blessings come. While you are waiting stay in God's will, don't make your situation worse by sinning. When God brings deliverance, you don't want to be trapped (You will have two challenges; the challenge of something new, and the problem you inflicted upon yourself). Sin is addicting and can become worse as you continue.

Whatever impurity you have God will cleanse off you as you repent (1 John 1:9). Judgement is reserved for your enemies and people that do wrong. Expect God to handle people and opposition. Avoid sin so you don't join God's judgement list.

God will protect you with a cloud by day, and guide you during the night seasons (Isaiah 4:5). God can guide you through the trials of life. Whatever difficulties you deal with in life there must be a time of rest and blessing.

13. Completion

1 Samuel 30:1-8 NIV. David and his men reached Ziklag on the third day. Now the Amalekites had raided the Negev and Ziklag. They had attacked Ziklag and burned it, 2 and had taken captive the women and everyone else in it, both young and old. They killed none of them, but carried them off as they went on their way.

The Amalekites only took the women captive. The devil cannot always kill what is yours, but he can hold things back. There are somethings you will obtain in your life that God may keep evidence of later. God's will is recorded in history within the Bible. People cannot change what God accomplished. Sometimes God permits people to do wrong to set an example for the next generation. When people are outside the will of God, they can suffer. This is a consequence of disobedience. People you know are watching you. God may use your failures as a lesson to them. It is better for you to learn something the hard way than for your family and friends to suffer because they were not taught.

3 When David and his men reached Ziklag, they found it destroyed by fire and their wives and sons and daughters taken captive. 4 So David and his men wept aloud until they had no strength left to weep. 5 David's two wives had been captured—Ahinoam of Jezreel and Abigail, the widow of Nabal of Carmel. 6 David was greatly distressed because the men were talking of stoning him; each one was bitter in spirit because of his sons and daughters. But David found strength in the LORD his God.

Find strength in God. Do not be bitter. Weep but do not be defeated. You are going to win. Believe God to restore anything the devil has taken from you or tried to ruin.

7 Then David said to Abiathar the priest, the son of Ahimelek, "Bring me the ephod." Abiathar brought it to him, 8 and David inquired of the LORD, "Shall I pursue this raiding party? Will I overtake them?"

"Pursue them," he answered. "You will certainly overtake them and succeed in the rescue."

Believe God for redemption and payback.

1. God can give guidance with ministry endeavours.

2. God can gradually increase your finances (Proverbs 13:11).

Whatever job you are at believe God for a higher income or to give you a new job with more pay.

Believe God for restoration. God is a God of justice. There are many instances in the Bible where the number three is used as the completion of something. In Genesis, the chief baker and the chief cupbearer both had dreams using the number three. The number three indicated the timing of three days in which the baker was impaled and the cupbearer was restored to his position (Gen 40:20-2).

Exodus mentions three annual festivals in a year. The festival of unleavened bread, the festival of harvest, and the festival of ingathering (Exodus 23:14-16).

Keep any biblical traditions and watch God bless you. This may be tithes, offering, or first fruit.

Matthew 12:40 explains that Jonah was in the belly of the whale three days and three nights and so will Jesus Christ be in the "heart of the earth." Believe to rise from whatever hardship you have had in the past. Jesus rose in three days (John 2: 19-22).

14. Prosperity

Believe God to bless you in three areas.

1. Relationships

God will give you favor in whatever circumstance you are in. Joseph had favor in sight of the keeper of the prison (Gen 39: 19-21). In difficult environments, God will send people to help you. Sometimes you must wait for the people God has you to be with.

Jacob did not appreciate Leah, so Rachel was made barren (Gen 29:26-31). Be sure to appreciate the people God places in your life but don't idolize them. Jacob had to wait for the woman he truly wanted.

2. Health

Forgiveness is an aid to good health. Holding anger against people can create sickness because anger can influence evil (Psalm 37:8). If you read the gospels of the New Testament the devil inflicts sickness through evil spirits in some cases.

Psalm 147:3 NIV *"He heals the brokenhearted, binding up their wounds."* God will bind up your wounds so you won't have to. Don't try to forget the pain of the past. Allow God to heal you rather.

3. Business endeavors and finances

The key to being successful and prosperous is in the Word of God (Joshua 1:8).

Proverbs 3:3-4 mentions that mercy and truth can gain favor in the sight of God and people. Mercy and truth are both godly qualities. Truth is found in the gospel of Jesus Christ (John 14:6). Mercy involves holding back punishment and forgiving (Psalm 51:1-2). Be kind to people who are not kind to you. Love everyone. God may use a person that you do not like to bless you.

God has wealth stored up for you but you must be able to handle it. Be patient when God increases you financially. Don't spend money that you do not have in your bank account when you can save up and pay for what you desire in full.

Ezekiel 7:3-7 KJV

3 Now is the end come upon thee, and I will send mine anger upon thee, and will judge thee according to thy ways, and will recompense upon thee all thine abominations.

Keep away from sin. God judges everyone so stay off the list of evil doers.

4 And mine eye shall not spare thee, neither will I have pity: but I will recompense thy ways upon thee, and thine abominations shall be in the midst of thee: and ye shall know that I am the LORD.

God will reveal to you your issues as you grow spiritually. Be willing to accept correction.

5 Thus saith the Lord GOD; An evil, an only evil, behold, is come.

6 An end is come, the end is come: it watcheth for thee; behold, it is come.

Whatever you are going through your end is watching for you. Keep serving God and staying faithful.

7 The morning is come unto thee, O thou that dwellest in the land: the time is come, the day of trouble is near, and not the sounding again of the mountains. We all desire to know God's timing. Usually the wait is not too long and not too short, but always makes sense afterwards. What God does in the background can come to the forefront in the blink of an eye.

15. Diligence

Ecclesiastes mentions that there is a time and a season for everything. God can teach you how to prioritize your time. You can have so much on your schedule that you don't know what to do first. Jesus worked his schedule around the people he ministered to. God can give you direction when you need to focus on one activity over another.

If you diligently hearken to what God commands, your health will be better (Exodus 15:26). Living godly involves eating and thinking godly. Believe God to heal you of any physical or mental turmoil you have experienced. God can restore concentration to you. Sometimes the cares of this world slow down your thought process. Expect God to renew your mind. He will help you think clearly. There are things we have anxiety about. This can be people coming and going, wanting more, the lack of a job, etc. Our prayers not only relieve us of anxiety but help us to receive a solution to our problem. Believe God for success in whatever environment you are in.

Diligence must be consistent until the end of a season (Hebrew 6:11). Keep the same focus beginning a task as you do when finishing a task.

Proverbs 10:4 NIV *"Lazy hands make for poverty, but diligent hands bring wealth."*

Be consistent and aim for quality in everything you do.

16. Promotion

Psalm 75 NRSV

1 We give thanks to you, O God;
*　we give thanks; your name is near.*
People tell of your wondrous deeds.

2 At the set time that I appoint
*　I will judge with equity.*
3 When the earth totters, with all its inhabitants,
*　it is I who keep its pillars steady. Selah*
4 I say to the boastful, "Do not boast,"
*　and to the wicked, "Do not lift up your horn;*
5 do not lift up your horn on high,
*　or speak with insolent neck."*

6 For not from the east or from the west
*　and not from the wilderness comes lifting up;*
7 but it is God who executes judgment,
*　putting down one and lifting up another.*

8 For in the hand of the LORD there is a cup
*　with foaming wine, well mixed;*
he will pour a draught from it,
*　and all the wicked of the earth*
*　shall drain it down to the dregs.*
9 But I will rejoice forever;
*　I will sing praises to the God of Jacob.*

10 All the horns of the wicked I will cut off,
but the horns of the righteous shall be exalted.

Thank the Lord for what he is about to do. Humility proceeds honor. People who boast will not prosper but those who keep a humble attitude will.

God has a set time for deliverance and it may have already begun for you. No matter what difficulties you are dealing with in life there is more God can do. Sometimes the biggest problem is the one that remains unsolved. There is a set time for God to bring deliverance to these types of issues. Keep believing and listening to the word you receive from God and expect a manifestation of it.

Waiting sometimes ends at an unexpected time. Hang on to your faith. Rewards are coming. Anything you have put up with for years and years will come to an end. Believe God to exalt you in the proper season.

17. Courage

Joshua 10:1-16 KJV Now it came to pass, when Adonizedek king of Jerusalem had heard how Joshua had taken Ai, and had utterly destroyed it; as he had done to Jericho and her king, so he had done to Ai and her king; and how the inhabitants of Gibeon had made peace with Israel, and were among them;

God can put you at peace with your enemies.

2 That they feared greatly, because Gibeon was a great city, as one of the royal cities, and because it was greater than Ai, and all the men thereof were mighty.

The trial seems greater than you but God has given you victory. Don't be afraid, God sees the people that bring evil upon you and he always has restoration, redemption, and resurrection power at hand. People need enemies to become stronger. There would be no triumph without a fight. The most important thing is winning.

3 Wherefore Adonizedek king of Jerusalem, sent unto Hoham king of Hebron, and unto Piram king of Jarmuth, and unto Japhia king of Lachish, and unto Debir king of Eglon, saying,

4 Come up unto me, and help me, that we may smite Gibeon: for it hath made peace with Joshua and with the children of Israel.

When people don't want to make peace with you God humbles them before your sight. Expect God to handle any people that oppose you.

5 Therefore the five kings of the Amorites, the king of Jerusalem, the king of Hebron, the king of Jarmuth, the king of Lachish, the king of Eglon, gathered themselves together, and went up, they and all their hosts, and encamped before Gibeon, and made war against it.

6 And the men of Gibeon sent unto Joshua to the camp to Gilgal, saying, Slack not thy hand from thy servants; come up to us quickly, and save us, and help us: for all the kings of the Amorites that dwell in the mountains are gathered together against us.

Expect God to show up in the next 90 days in whatever area you are waiting. God can answer you in two ways; by acting on the issue, or by pointing you in the right direction for your deliverance to happen. Answers to prayer always cause deliverance whether immediate or after a waiting period.

Mountains are often climbed over. When a mountain is moved, you miss the strength increase. Climbing teaches you endurance.

7 So Joshua ascended from Gilgal, he, and all the people of war with him, and all the mighty men of valour.

You are made in God's image. Use your mouth as a sword. Be confident not fearful.

8 And the LORD said unto Joshua, Fear them not: for I have delivered them into thine hand; there shall not a man of them stand before thee.

Anyone working against you receiving breakthrough will be humbled. God can push people out of the way so your plans will prosper. Righteousness leads to eternal life and light overcomes darkness. Believe God to shed light on your circumstances.

People who are wise in their own eyes always come to shame (Proverbs 3:7). Some people live good lives on earth but when they die their riches are gone and they go to hell. God deals with all evil although we don't always know when.

11 And it came to pass, as they fled from before Israel, and were in the going down to Bethhoron, that the LORD cast down great stones from heaven upon them unto Azekah, and they died: they were more which died with hailstones than they whom the children of Israel slew with the sword.

12 Then spake Joshua to the LORD in the day when the LORD delivered up the Amorites before the children of Israel, and he said in the sight of Israel, Sun, stand thou still upon Gibeon; and thou, Moon, in the valley of Ajalon.

13 And the sun stood still, and the moon stayed, until the people had avenged themselves upon their enemies. Is not this written in the book of Jasher? So the sun stood still in the midst of heaven, and hasted not to go down about a whole day.

The Word of God is a sword in the Bible (Ephesians 6:17). Use the power of your words. By doing this you tap into God's creative power.

14 And there was no day like that before it or after it, that the LORD hearkened unto the voice of a man: for the LORD fought for Israel.

God is obligated to perform anything you say within his will.

If you are unable to fight Jesus will fight for you. Keep still. God never lets his people be ashamed for believing him. He will counterattack any attacks that come to you. When you read the Bible the righteous always win in the end. That's why Jesus triumphed over death. Whatever your struggling with he will fight for you when you can't.

15 And Joshua returned, and all Israel with him, unto the camp to Gilgal.

16 But these five kings fled, and hid themselves in a cave at Makkedah.

God can deal with your enemies so well they will flee from you. Keep a humble attitude. *"The wicked flee when no man pursueth: but the righteous are bold as a lion"* (Proverbs 28:1 KJV). Think of God as the lion, you have his boldness. He hunts down your enemies for you while you stay in place for victory. Your courage is in waiting within the will of God.

18. Renewal

Romans 12: 1-2 NIV Therefore, I urge you, brothers and sisters, in view of God's mercy, to offer your bodies as a living sacrifice, holy and pleasing to God—this is your true and proper worship. 2 Do not conform to the pattern of this world, but be transformed by the renewing of your mind. Then you will be able to test and approve what God's will is—his good, pleasing and perfect will.

You must be holy and pleasing to God by avoiding sin. God deserves praise every day you wake up. You'll notice an increase in his presence and a greater awareness of what he is doing in your life. Worship aids in getting answers to prayer. If you want to know what the next step is in your life worshiping can help.

God wants to reign in your mind and give you peace (Isaiah 26:3). If your mindset isn't right you will have a bad mood every time you encounter a trial in life. When you get out of this trial something else will happen to bring you down. God wants you to have constant peace in his presence. If you can approve what God's will is in your life, rest is in believing him to act. Disappointment comes when you believe God for something that takes long to occur. If you're in a situation that you know you don't belong in or is not God's will, expect him to bring you out. The plans of God always end in a way that is pleasing to him even if you don't live to see the outcome. Heaven is life beyond death so we have assurance of God's will and presence beyond life on earth.

Ask and it will be given to you, seek and you will find, knock and the door will be opened to you (Matthew 7:7 NIV).

God has keys to all the doors you can't open. Keep knocking and answers will come whether through circumstance, a scripture, or a person.

> *Romans 12:21 NIV Do not be overcome by evil, but overcome evil with good.*

Sometimes the afflictions that happen to us are undeserved. Job was consistently righteous so the devil had to ask for permission from God to afflict him. When you live righteously you don't give the devil a specific reason to afflict you. Obviously sin and disobedience to God can further invite the devil to attack you. A righteous life makes evil doers look bad. Evildoers deserve the vengeance that God has reserved for them so it becomes part of his righteousness. God's righteousness involves repaying and making things fair. God can repay you for every unfair thing that happens. Believe God to make up for any misfortune you have encountered because he is able.

Believe God to:

1. Repay for the unrighteous deeds of others.
2. Deal with slanderers and persecutors.
3. Restore things to people who have lost them.

-God will heal those who have had a broken heart.

-God will reward people according to their good works.

-God will give people the desires of their heart.

19. Harvest

Proverbs 11 KJV

1 A false balance is abomination to the LORD: but a just weight is his delight.
The righteous are a just weight. God will bless righteous living.

2 When pride cometh, then cometh shame: but with the lowly is wisdom.
We need wisdom to obtain some things. God will grant it.

3 The integrity of the upright shall guide them: but the perverseness of transgressors shall destroy them.

We don't need to handle our enemies. Their own perverseness judges them.

4 Riches profit not in the day of wrath: but righteousness delivereth from death.

Our trial is a day of wrath, but righteousness will deliver us.

5 The righteousness of the perfect shall direct his way: but the wicked shall fall by his own wickedness.

People reap what they sow, don't plot vengeance.

7 When a wicked man dieth, his expectation shall perish: and the hope of unjust men perisheth. The righteous is delivered out of trouble, and the wicked cometh in his stead.

Evil deeds always have a consequence. Do not compare yourself or be jealous of others. God delivers us out of trouble and can fulfill the desires of our hearts.

9 An hypocrite with his mouth destroyeth his neighbour: but through knowledge shall the just be delivered.

Our knowledge delivers us. Use the knowledge you have while you seek God for more. God speaks to our souls with knowledge. When you receive discernment of how to handle a specific situation the knowledge is coming from God.

Wisdom is in the heart, which determines the thoughts you have (Proverbs 2:10, Genesis 6:5, Matthew 15:19). Let the word of God become a part of your heart and your thought life will become more like God.

20. Payback

Proverbs 24:12 KJV "If you say, "But we knew nothing about this," does not he who weighs the heart perceive it? Does not he who guards your life know it? Will he not repay everyone according to what they have done?

God will repay evil deeds. Do not be discouraged.

16 for though the righteous fall seven times, they rise again, but the wicked stumble when calamity strikes.

God can allow you to fall seven times, but the eighth time you will rise.

17-8 Do not gloat when your enemy falls; when they stumble, do not let your heart rejoice, or the LORD will see and disapprove and turn his wrath away from them.

Expect God's vengeance on your enemies but don't wish evil upon them.

Proverbs 24: 19-22 Do not fret because of evildoers or be envious of the wicked, for the evildoer has no future hope, and the lamp of the wicked will be snuffed out. Fear the Lord and the king, my son, and do not join with rebellious officials, for those two will send sudden destruction on them, and who knows what calamities they can bring?

Treasures gotten by wicked deeds dry out. Defeat isn't coming to you but whoever deserves it. People who are a bad influence are contagious, be careful who you associate yourself with. People who follow the worlds standards and not biblical standards should not be an influence in your life. Don't adjust to the trends of culture if they contradict the Bible.

There are three principles you should believe:

1. Don't hate your enemies.

2. Your offender(s) are not getting away with anything.

3. God will judge anyone who attempts to hinder or harm you.

Author Bio:

Nathaniel E. Jones is a Master of Theology graduate from Palmer Theological Seminary. He has worked with various ministries within Southern New Jersey and Pennsylvania. Nathaniel enjoys teaching the Bible and occasionally preaches. He has done ministry the past 7 years working with mid-age adults to elderly people.

20 Promises with Biblical Proof by
Nathaniel E. Jones

www.ingramcontent.com/pod-product-compliance
Lightning Source LLC
Chambersburg PA
CBHW031218090426
42736CB00009B/965